RECIPES

A SIMPLE COCKTAIL BOOK

Cocktail

....

Creator .... Date

Ingredients:

....
....
....
....
....   Garnish
....

Method

....
....
....
....
....

Glass

Note

....
....
....

Cocktail

....

Creator .... Date

Ingredients: ....

....

....

....

....   Garnish

....

Method

....

....

....

....

....

Glass

Note

....

....

....

Cocktail

....

Creator .... Date ....

Ingredients: ....

....
....
....
....   Garnish
....

Method

....
....
....
....
....
....

Glass

Note

....
....
....

Cocktail

....

Creator .... Date

Ingredients:

....
....
....
....   Garnish
....

Method

....
....
....
....
....

Glass

Note

....
....
....

Cocktail

....

Creator .... Date ....

Ingredients: ....

....

....

....

....   Garnish

....

Method

....

....

....

....

....

Glass

Note

....

....

....

Cocktail

....

Creator .... Date ....

Ingredients: ....

....
....
....
.... Garnish
....

Method

....
....
....
....
....

Glass

Note

....
....
....

Cocktail

....

Creator .... Date ....

Ingredients: ....

....
....
....
....
....   Garnish
                                              ....

Method

....
....
....
....
....
....

Glass

Note

....
....
....

Cocktail

....

Creator .... Date

Ingredients: ....

....
....
....
....
....   Garnish
....

Method

....
....
....
....
....
....

Glass

Note

....
....
....

Cocktail

....

Creator .... Date

Ingredients: ....

....
....
....
....
....   Garnish
....

Method

....
....
....
....
....

Glass

Note

....
....
....

Cocktail

....

Creator .... Date ....

Ingredients: ·················

....
....
....
....
....   Garnish

Method

....
....
....
....
....

Glass

Note

....
....
....

Cocktail

....

Creator .... Date ....

Ingredients: ················

....

....

....

....

.... Garnish

....

Method

....

....

....

....

....

Glass

Note

....

....

....

Cocktail

....

Creator .... Date ....

Ingredients: ....

....	....
....	....
....	....
....	Garnish
....	

Method

....

....

....

....

....

Glass

Note

....

....

....

Cocktail

....

Creator .... Date ....

Ingredients: ....

....

....

....

....

.... Garnish

....

Method

....

....

....

....

....

Glass

Note

....

....

....

Cocktail

....

Creator .... Date

Ingredients: ....

....
....
....
.... Garnish
....

Method

....
....
....
....
....

Glass

Note

....
....
....

Cocktail

....

Creator .... Date

Ingredients: ....

....
....
....
....
....   Garnish
                                             ....

Method

....
....
....
....
....
....

Glass

Note

....
....
....

Cocktail

....

Creator .... Date

Ingredients: ·················

....
....
....
....
....   Garnish
....

Method

....
....
....
....
....
....

Glass

Note

....
....
....

Cocktail

....

Creator .... Date ....

Ingredients: ....

....

....

....

....   Garnish

....

Method

....

....

....

....

....

Glass

Note

....

....

....

Cocktail

....

Creator .... Date

Ingredients: ....

....
....
....
....   Garnish
....

Method

....
....
....
....
....

Glass

Note

....
....
....

Cocktail

....

Creator .... Date

Ingredients: ....

....
....
....
....
....   Garnish

Method

....
....
....
....
....

Glass

Note

....
....
....

Cocktail

....

Creator .... Date

Ingredients: ....

....
....
....
....
                                              Garnish

Method

....
....
....
....
....

Glass

Note

....
....
....

Cocktail

....

Creator .... Date ....

Ingredients: ....

....
....
....
....
....   Garnish
                                                         ....

Method

....

....

....

....

....

....

Glass

Note

....

....

....

Cocktail

....

Creator .... Date

Ingredients: ....

....
....
....
....
.... Garnish
....

Method

....
....
....
....
....

Glass

Note

....
....
....

Cocktail

....

Creator .... Date

Ingredients: ....

....
....
....
....   Garnish
....

Method

....
....
....
....
....

Glass

Note

....
....
....

Cocktail

....

Creator .... Date ....

Ingredients: · · · · · · · · · · · · · · · ·

....

....

....

....   Garnish

....

Method

....

....

....

....

....

....

Glass

Note

....

....

....

Cocktail

....

Creator .... Date ....

Ingredients: ....

....
....
....
....
.... **Garnish**
....

Method

....
....
....
....
....
....

Glass

Note

....
....
....

Cocktail

....

Creator .... Date ....

Ingredients: ....

....
....
....
.... Garnish
....

Method

....
....
....
....
....
....

Glass

Note

....
....
....

Cocktail

....

Creator .... Date ....

Ingredients: ·················

....

....

....

....   Garnish

....

Method

....

....

....

....

....

....

Glass

Note

....

....

....

Cocktail

....

Creator .... Date

Ingredients: ....

....
....
....
.... Garnish
....

Method

....
....
....
....
....

Glass

Note

....
....
....

Cocktail

....

Creator .... Date ....

Ingredients: ....

....
....
....
....
....   Garnish
....

Method

....
....
....
....
....
....

Glass

Note

....
....
....

Cocktail

....

Creator .... Date

· ·Ingredients· · · · · · · · · · · · · · · ·

....

....

....

....   Garnish

....

Method

....

....

....

....

....

Glass

Note

....

....

....

Cocktail

....

Creator .... Date

· Ingredients · ·············

....
....
....
....   Garnish

Method

....
....
....
....
....

Glass

Note

....
....
....

Cocktail

....

Creator .... Date

Ingredients: ....

....
....
....
.... Garnish
....

Method

....
....
....
....
....
....

Glass

Note

....
....
....

Cocktail

....

Creator .... Date ....

Ingredients: ....

....
....
....
.... Garnish
....

Method

....
....
....
....
....

Glass

Note

....
....
....

Cocktail

....

Creator .... Date

Ingredients: ....

.... | ....
.... | ....
.... | ....
.... | Garnish
.... | ....

Method

....
....
....
....
....

Glass

Note

....
....
....

Cocktail

....

Creator .... Date

Ingredients: ....

....
....
....
....   Garnish
....

Method

....
....
....
....
....

Glass

Note

....
....
....

Cocktail

....

Creator .... Date ....

Ingredients ....

....
....
....
....
                                                 Garnish
                                                 ....

Method

....
....
....
....
....
....

Glass

Note

....
....
....

Cocktail

....

Creator .... Date ....

Ingredients: ·················

....	....
....	....
....	....
....	Garnish
....	....

Method

....

....

....

....

....

Glass

Note

....

....

....

Cocktail

....

Creator .... Date

Ingredients ....

....
....
....
....
....   Garnish
....

Method

....
....
....
....
....

Glass

Note

....
....
....

Cocktail

....

Creator .... Date ....

Ingredients: ....

....

....

....

....   Garnish

....

Method

....

....

....

....

....

Glass

Note

....

....

....

Cocktail

....

Creator .... Date

Ingredients: ....

....
....
....
....
....   Garnish
                                               ....

Method

....
....
....
....
....

Glass

Note

....
....
....

Cocktail

....

Creator .... Date

Ingredients: ....

....
....
....
....
....   Garnish

Method

....
....
....
....
....

Glass

Note

....
....
....

Cocktail

....

Creator .... Date ....

Ingredients: ....

....
....
....
....
.... Garnish
....

Method

....
....
....
....
....

Glass

Note

....
....
....

Cocktail

....

Creator .... Date

··Ingredients:················

....
....
....
....
.... Garnish
....

Method

....
....
....
....
....

Glass

Note

....
....
....

Cocktail

....

Creator .... Date ....

Ingredients ....

....
....
....
....
....   Garnish
....

Method

....
....
....
....
....
....

Glass

Note

....
....
....

Cocktail

....

Creator .... Date ....

Ingredients: ....

....

....

....

....   Garnish

....

Method

....

....

....

....

....

Glass

Note

....

....

....

Cocktail

....

Creator .... Date

Ingredients

.... | ....
.... | ....
.... | ....
.... | ....
.... | Garnish
.... | ....

Method

....
....
....
....
....

Glass

Note

....
....
....

Cocktail

....

Creator .... Date ....

Ingredients ....

....
....
....
....   Garnish
....

Method

....
....
....
....
....
....

Glass

Note

....
....
....

Cocktail

....

Creator .... Date

Ingredients: ....

....
....
....
.... Garnish
....

Method

....
....
....
....
....
....

Glass

Note

....
....
....

Cocktail

....

Creator .... Date ....

Ingredients:

....
....
....
....
....   Garnish
....

Method

....
....
....
....
....

Glass

Note

....
....
....

Cocktail

....

Creator .... Date

Ingredients: ....

....
....
....
....
....   Garnish

Method

....
....
....
....
....

Glass

Note

....
....
....

Cocktail

....

Creator .... Date

Ingredients: ....

....

....

....

....

....   Garnish

                              ....

Method

....

....

....

....

....

....

Glass

Note

....

....

....

Cocktail

....

Creator .... Date

Ingredients: ....

....
....
....
....
....   Garnish
                                                  ....

Method

....
....
....
....
....

Glass

Note

....
....
....

Cocktail

....

Creator .... Date

Ingredients:

....
....
....
....   Garnish
....

Method

....
....
....
....
....

Glass

Note

....
....
....

Cocktail

....

Creator .... Date ....

Ingredients ....

....
....
....
....
.... Garnish
....

Method

....
....
....
....
....
....

Glass

Note

....
....
....

Cocktail

....

Creator .... Date ....

Ingredients: ....

....

....

....

....   Garnish

....

Method

....

....

....

....

....

Glass

Note

....

....

....

Cocktail

....

Creator .... Date

Ingredients: ....

....
....
....
....
.... Garnish
....

Method

....
....
....
....
....

Glass

Note

....
....
....

Cocktail

....

Creator .... Date ....

Ingredients: ....

....
....
....
....
.... Garnish
....

Method

....
....
....
....
....
....

Glass

Note

....
....
....

Cocktail

....

Creator .... Date

Ingredients: ....

....
....
....
....   Garnish
....

Method

....
....
....
....
....

Glass

Note

....
....
....

Cocktail

....

Creator .... Date ....

Ingredients: ·················

....
....
....
....
....   Garnish
                                                     ....

Method

....
....
....
....
....

Glass

Note

....
....
....

Cocktail

....

Creator .... Date

Ingredients: ....

.... | ....
.... | ....
.... | ....
.... |
.... | Garnish
.... | ....

Method

....

....

....

....

....

Glass

Note

....

....

....

Cocktail

....

Creator .... Date

·Ingredients· ················

....
....
....
....
.... Garnish
....

Method

....
....
....
....
....

Glass

Note

....
....
....

Cocktail

....

Creator .... Date ....

Ingredients: ....

....	....
....	....
....	....
....	Garnish
....	....

Method

....

....

....

....

....

Glass

Note

....

....

....

Cocktail

....

Creator .... Date ....

Ingredients: ·················

....
....
....
....   Garnish
....

Method

....
....
....
....
....
....

Glass

Note

....
....
....

Cocktail

....

Creator .... Date

Ingredients ....

....
....
....
....
....   Garnish
....

Method

....
....
....
....
....

Glass

Note

....
....
....

Cocktail

....

Creator .... Date

Ingredients: ....

....

....

....

.... Garnish

....

Method

....

....

....

....

....

Glass

Note

....

....

....

Cocktail

....

Creator .... Date

Ingredients: ....

....
....
....
....
.... Garnish
....

Method

....
....
....
....
....

Glass

Note

....
....
....

Cocktail

....

Creator .... Date

Ingredients: ....

....

....

....

.... Garnish

....

Method

....

....

....

....

....

Glass

Note

....

....

....

Cocktail

....

Creator .... Date

·Ingredients· ·················

....
....
....
....   Garnish
....

Method

....
....
....
....
....

Glass

Note

....
....
....

Cocktail

....

Creator .... Date ....

Ingredients: ....

....
....
....
.... Garnish
....

Method

....
....
....
....
....
....

Glass

Note

....
....
....

Cocktail

....

Creator .... Date

Ingredients: ....

....
....
....
....   Garnish
                                            ....

Method

....
....
....
....
....

Glass

Note

....
....
....

Cocktail

....

Creator .... Date

Ingredients: ....

....
....
....
....   Garnish
....

Method

....
....
....
....
....
....

Glass

Note

....
....
....

Cocktail

....

Creator .... Date

Ingredients: ....

....

....

....

....   Garnish

....

Method

....

....

....

....

....

Glass

Note

....

....

....

Cocktail

....

Creator .... Date

Ingredients: ....

....
....
....
.... Garnish
....

Method

....
....
....
....
....
....

Glass

Note

....
....
....

Cocktail

....

Creator .... Date

Ingredients: ....

....

....

....

....

.... Garnish

....

Method

....

....

....

....

....

Glass

Note

....

....

....

Cocktail

....

Creator .... Date

Ingredients: ....

....

....

....

....   Garnish
....

Method

....

....

....

....

....

Glass

Note

....

....

....

Cocktail

....

Creator .... Date

Ingredients: ·················

....
....
....
....
.... Garnish
....

Method

....
....
....
....
....

Glass

Note

....
....
....

Cocktail

....

Creator .... Date

Ingredients: ....

....
....
....
....   Garnish
                                                 ....

Method

....
....
....
....
....

Glass

Note

....
....
....

Cocktail

....

Creator .... Date ....

Ingredients: ....

....
....
....
....
.... Garnish
....

Method

....
....
....
....
....

Glass

Note

....
....
....

Cocktail

....

Creator .... Date

Ingredients: ....

....
....
....
.... Garnish
....

Method

....
....
....
....
....
....

Glass

Note

....
....
....

Cocktail

....

Creator .... Date ....

··Ingredients; ················

....

....

....

.... Garnish
....

Method

....

....

....

....

Glass

Note

....

....

....

Cocktail

....

Creator .... Date

Ingredients ·················

....
....
....
....
....   Garnish
                                                           ....

Method

....
....
....
....
....

Glass

Note

....
....
....

Cocktail

....

Creator .... Date

Ingredients: ....

....	....
....	....
....	....
....	Garnish
	....

Method

....
....
....
....
....

Glass

Note

....
....
....

Cocktail

....

Creator .... Date

·Ingredients· ··············

....

....

....

....   Garnish

....

Method

....

....

....

....

....

....

Glass

Note

....

....

....

Cocktail

....

Creator .... Date

Ingredients: ....

....
....
....
....   Garnish
                                               ....

Method

....
....
....
....
....

Glass

Note

....
....
....

Cocktail

....

Creator .... Date ....

Ingredients: ·······················

....
....
....
....   Garnish
....

Method

....
....
....
....
....
....

Glass

Note

....
....
....

Cocktail

....

Creator .... Date

Ingredients: ....

....

....

....

.... Garnish

....

Method

....

....

....

....

....

Glass

Note

....

....

....

Cocktail

....

Creator .... Date ....

Ingredients: ················

....

....

....

....   Garnish

....

Method

....

....

....

....

....

Glass

Note

....

....

....

Cocktail

....

Creator .... Date ....

Ingredients: ....

....
....
....
....   Garnish
....

Method

....
....
....
....
....
....

Glass

Note

....
....
....

Cocktail

....

Creator .... Date

Ingredients: ....

....
....
....
....   Garnish

Method

....
....
....
....
....

Glass

Note

....
....
....

Cocktail

....

Creator .... Date

Ingredients: ....

....
....
....
....
....

....
....
....

Garnish
....

Method

....
....
....
....

Glass

Note

....
....
....

Cocktail

....

Creator .... Date ....

·Ingredients· ·············

....

....

....

....   Garnish

....

Method

....

....

....

....

....

....

Glass

Note

....

....

....

Cocktail

....

Creator .... Date

Ingredients: ....

....
....
....
....   Garnish
....

Method

....
....
....
....
....

Glass

Note

....
....
....

Cocktail

....

Creator .... Date

Ingredients: ·················

....

....

....

....   Garnish

Method

....

....

....

....

....

Glass

Note

....

....

....

Cocktail

....

Creator .... Date ....

Ingredients: ....

....

....

....

....   Garnish

....

Method

....

....

....

....

....

Glass

Note

....

....

....

Cocktail

....

Creator .... Date

·Ingredients· ···············

....	....
....	....
....	....
....	Garnish
	....

Method

....
....
....
....
....
....

Glass

Note

....
....
....

Cocktail

....

Creator .... Date

Ingredients: ....

....
....
....
....   Garnish
....

Method

....
....
....
....
....

Glass

Note

....
....
....

Cocktail

....

Creator .... Date ....

··Ingredients: ················

....
....
....
....   Garnish
....

Method

....
....
....
....
....

Glass

Note

....
....
....

Cocktail

....

Creator .... Date

Ingredients: ....

.... | ....
.... | ....
.... | ....
.... | Garnish
.... | ....

Method

....
....
....
....
....

Glass

Note

....
....
....

Cocktail

....

Creator .... Date

Ingredients: ....

....
....
....
....
....   Garnish
                                                  ....

Method

....
....
....
....
....
....

Glass

Note

....
....
....

Cocktail

....

Creator .... Date ....

Ingredients: ....

....

....

....

....   Garnish

....

Method

....

....

....

....

....

Glass

Note

....

....

....

Cocktail

....

Creator .... Date

·· Ingredients: ················

....
....
....
....   Garnish
....

Method

....
....
....
....
....

Glass

Note

....
....
....

Cocktail

....

Creator .... Date ....

Ingredients:

....
....
....
....

Garnish
....

Method

....
....
....
....
....

Glass

Note

....
....
....

Cocktail

....

Creator .... Date ....

Ingredients ....

....
....
....
....   Garnish
....

Method

....
....
....
....
....

Glass

Note

....
....
....

Cocktail

....

Creator .... Date

·Ingredients:···············

....
....
....
....   Garnish
....

Method

....
....
....
....
....

Glass

Note

....
....
....

Cocktail

....

Creator .... Date

·Ingredients· · · · · · · · · · · · · ·

....

....

....

....   Garnish

....

Method

....

....

....

....

....

Glass

Note

....

....

....

Cocktail

....

Creator .... Date

Ingredients: ·················

....	....
....	....
....	....
....	Garnish
....	....

Method

....
....
....
....
....

Glass

Note

....
....
....

Cocktail

....

Creator .... Date

Ingredients: ·····················

....
....
....
....   Garnish
                                      ....

Method

....
....
....
....
....

Glass

Note

....
....
....

Cocktail

....

Creator .... Date ....

Ingredients: ....

....
....
....
....   Garnish
....

Method

....
....
....
....
....
....

Glass

Note

....
....
....

Cocktail

....

Creator .... Date

Ingredients: ....

....

....

....

....   Garnish

Method

....

....

....

....

....

Glass

Note

....

....

....

Cocktail

....

Creator .... Date

Ingredients: ....

....
....
....
....
                        Garnish
                        ....

Method

....
....
....
....
....

Glass

Note

....
....
....

Cocktail

....

Creator .... Date

Ingredients: ·················

....
....
....
....
                                                Garnish
                                                ....

Method

....
....
....
....
....

Glass

Note

....
....
....

Cocktail

....

Creator .... Date ....

Ingredients: ....

....
....
....
....   Garnish
....

Method

....
....
....
....
....

Glass

Note

....
....
....

Cocktail

....

Creator .... Date

Ingredients: ....

....
....
....
.... Garnish
....

Method

....
....
....
....
....

Glass

Note

....
....
....

Cocktail

....

Creator .... Date ....

Ingredients: ....

.... | ....
.... | ....
.... | ....
.... |
.... | Garnish
.... | ....

Method

....
....
....
....
....
....

Glass

Note

....
....
....

Cocktail

....

Creator .... Date ....

Ingredients: ....

....

....

....

.... Garnish

....

Method

....

....

....

....

....

....

Glass

Note

....

....

....

Cocktail

....

Creator .... Date ....

Ingredients: ....

....	....
....	....
....	....
....	Garnish
....	....

Method

....
....
....
....
....

Glass

Note

....
....
....

Cocktail

....

Creator .... Date

Ingredients: ....

....	....
....	....
....	....
....	Garnish
	....

Method

....

....

....

....

....

....

Glass

Note

....

....

....

Cocktail

....

Creator .... Date ....

··Ingredients: ················

.... | ....
.... | ....
.... | ....
.... |
.... | Garnish
.... | ....

Method

....
....
....
....
....

Glass

Note

....
....
....

Cocktail

....

Creator .... Date

Ingredients ....

....

....

....

....

                                              Garnish
                                              ....

Method

....

....

....

....

....

....

Glass

Note

....

....

....

Cocktail

....

Creator .... Date

Ingredients: ....

....
....
....
....   Garnish
....

Method

....
....
....
....
....

Glass

Note

....
....
....

Printed in Great Britain
by Amazon